Baby Animals

Cody Keiser

INFOMAX COMMON CORE READERS

Rosen Classroom™

New York

Published in 2013 by The Rosen Publishing Group, Inc.
29 East 21st Street, New York, NY 10010

Book Design: Michael Harmon

Photo Credits: Cover Alan Jeffery/Shutterstock.com; p. 5 Mogens Trolle/Shutterstock.com;
p. 7 Albie Venter/Shutterstock.com; p. 9 Dave Pusey/Shutterstock.com;
p. 11 (mallards) Andrejs Jegorovs/Shutterstock.com;
p. 11 (duckling) Dominik Spolitino/Photographer's Choice/Getty Images;
p. 13 (frog) ponsuwan/Shutterstock.com; p. 13 (tadpole) Turchina Natalia/Shutterstock.com;
p. 15 Petr Masek/Shutterstock.com.

ISBN: 978-1-4488-8923-5
6-pack ISBN: 978-1-4488-8924-2

Manufactured in the United States of America

CPSIA Compliance Information: Batch #WS12RC: For further information contact Rosen Publishing, New York, New York at 1-800-237-9932.

Word Count: 48

Contents

A lion is big.
A cub is small.

An elephant is tall.
A calf is short.

A zebra has a long tail.
A foal has a short tail.

A duck flies.
A duckling walks.

A frog hops.
A tadpole swims.

A pig is large.
A piglet is little.

Words to Know

duckling

foal

piglet

tadpole

Index